Please Stand Back From The Platform Door

Vishal Nanda

Proverse Hong Kong

18 November 2021

PLEASE STAND BACK FROM THE PLATFORM DOOR contains slices of perspectives in a great big place. But the writer contends that these perspectives are held by others as well, that others have felt them, that they resonate through Hong Kong and into other cities, and other disconnected, disjointed individuals on other trains on their way to other stations.

The writer hopes that you will find something inside that you can relate to, that you can feel something about. He hopes by the end of it you will have had some kind of view into or out of a window, despite being on a train underground. A glimpse into the mind of a Hong Konger, one among seven million others.

"We might agree on some things and disagree on others", writes Vishal Nanda, "but by the end we would have traveled together, and that is enough to make acquaintances of us both, which is quite alright by me."

VISHAL NANDA is in all respects a "third-culture kid". Ethnically Indian, he is the second generation of his family to be born in Hong Kong. He attended an international school in Hong Kong and then attended the University of York in the UK, graduating with a BA (Hons) in English and Related Literature.

He returned to Hong Kong, where he has taught creative writing, tutored English language and literature (specialising in the IB, GCSE and A levels), and worked as an indie roleplaying and video game designer for several companies, including Xbox live and mobile.

Vishal has family in the UK and for the past five years prior to the Covid-19 pandemic, has attended the Edinburgh Fringe Festival.

A published poet, he is a member of the Hong Kong Peel Street Poets, performing poetry at their events since 2014, and winning the group's Poetry Slam Competition in 2019. He has additionally performed spoken word poetry at the Hong Kong International Literary Festival, TEDx events, and on radio at RTHK3, among others.

Supported by

Hong Kong Arts Development Council fully supports freedom of artistic expression. The views and opinions expressed in this project do not represent the stand of the Council.

PLEASE STAND BACK FROM THE PLATFORM DOOR

Vishal Nanda

A Proverse Prize Finalist 2020

Proverse Hong Kong

Please Stand Back From The Platform Door
By Vishal Nanda
First published in Hong Kong
by Proverse Hong Kong,
under sole and exclusive right and licence,
18 November 2021.
Paperback: ISBN 13: 978-988-8492-44-2
Alternate Paperback Edition: ISBN 13: 978-988-8492-45-9
Ebook: ISBN 13: 978-988-8492-46-6

Distribution (Hong Kong and worldwide)
The Chinese University of Hong Kong Press,
The Chinese University of Hong Kong,
Shatin, New Territories, Hong Kong SAR.
Email: cup@cuhk.edu.hk; Web: www.cup.cuhk.edu.hk
Distribution (United Kingdom)
Stephen Inman, Worcester, UK.
Enquiries to Proverse Hong Kong
P.O. Box 259, Tung Chung Post Office,
Lantau, NT, Hong Kong SAR, China.
Email: proverse@netvigator.com;
Web: www.proversepublishing.com

Cover photo, courtesy Roman Olinchuk.
Cover design by Artist Hong Kong.

British Library Cataloguing in Publication Data
A catalogue record for the first paperback edition
is available from the British Library

Acknowledgements

I have the urge to thank a great many people, who throughout my life have propped me up with their faith and encouragement and told me in so many ways that what I wrote was worth being read. I would not want to miss a single person out, from my school teachers, Miss Ritchie, Miss Hannaford, Mr Mayers, to my old friends, Jennifer, Long, Azra, Jaimee, Ben, Jason, Steven, Kevin, and Henrik, to my other friends, who hold me in varying levels of esteem, Fran, Karen, and Sam, to my publishers and the founders of the Proverse Prize: Gillian and Verner Bickley, to all the Peel Street Poets, my family and to Becca, finally and most of all.

But that doesn't do it justice. I would need to write another book, including all the names I left out, a much better book, with nothing but detailed thanks, the series of events, the words they said that have been soldered to my heart, and the countless moments where they believed in me when so often I did not believe in myself. Indeed, I have decided that this is the most important page of the book, because whatever the collection's merits or flaws, these people that I am so blessed to have known, have helped with its creation, and isn't that kind of neat? They loved me into existence too, because they so often told me that I was a writer, regardless of whether I felt otherwise. So thank you, one and all, for every ounce of support and every minute of your time. I am the sum of your influences, and so are my poems.

To Becca,
To the Moon and back,
Forever and always

Author's Introduction

As the title "Please Stand Back From the Platform Door" suggests, I intend my collection to be an urban journey through a mental, physical and spiritual space, and one that I hope others have also undertaken in their own way. The publication of this journey will hopefully resonate with those in Hong Kong and abroad.

It is challenging to state exactly what aspirations I have as an artist, and how to consciously understand them myself, let alone communicate them to another person. I can say that art stems from an individual's voice, but hopefully also as a representation of a whole, even if that demographic is not easily defined through ethnicity, gender or age.

I hope that my poetry speaks for more than just myself, and represents instead a sector of Hong Kong's English speaking population which may not be fully represented in the arts at the present. I am a native-born, ethnically Indian, British-passport-holding permanent resident of Hong Kong. I am both a local and a foreigner in my own country. But I am also not from anywhere else—this is my home, and my memories, loves, setbacks and indeed, aspirations are wrapped up only here, only in Hong Kong, and not in any other native land that I might return to.

There are others like me, usually identifying under the umbrella of the "third culture kid". But in my heart of hearts, I know I am a Hong Konger. I am not sure what that means, except to say that the poems I have written are from the point of view of a Hong Konger, though one that is filtered through privilege, third-culture-kid (TCK) values, English-speaking, an ethnic Indian background and the colonial detritus that passes it in its wake.

I do not know whether what I say is identifiable for the average Hong Konger, but I would argue that such a demographic (i.e. "the average Hong Konger") does not exist, because Hong Kong is a place of variety, with a myriad of ethnic groups, social strata, geographical microcosms and gender, age and neurological conditions.

So as a Hong Konger, I hope that the words of a local, in my own right, even if not in the majorities' right, have value, and speak to those who grew up here and abroad as well, whether as local or foreign. If the poems speak with any semblance of universality I will be greatly satisfied.

In truth, there is one demographic I would like to speak to more than any other, that is the non-neurotypical, who experience mental health issues in our city. My poems are filled with experiences of anxiety, alienation, disconnection and, I'd like to think, hope and reconciliation.

If my poems reach another person who experiences a similar loneliness or isolation, or questions their own experiences and struggles with stress, anxiety and mental health, then I will have succeeded.

I myself am not neurotypical, but bipolar, and thus from a minority that is not well represented in poetry at the moment, and deserves a voice, to add to the chorus of Hong Kong citizens and contribute another facet to the city's identity. But on the other hand, I think that my poems are also about those who face more universal challenges, perhaps ones that can be found throughout modern living, throughout urban living, through navigating the world at this technological crossroads.

My hopes are to connect with people from all these sectors and more. To have a voice where there is otherwise silence, or to add to the great conversation that better writers than me have started and contributed towards.

If there is merit to some of my work, then I believe there is merit to its existing in a more widely distributed form. At times, my poems are not about the beauty of Hong Kong, or of any utopian ideal, but of sickness and desperation. Too often, we are afraid to speak of that which troubles us, or are even able to articulate it in the first place. But more so than celebrating the beauty of the world around us, which there is obvious merit in, I believe that speaking for those who suffer silently may, at the least, highlight issues that others may not have thought existed, and at best, provide solace, camaraderie, and hope to others.

Vishal Nanda
Hong Kong

CONTENTS

Acknowledgements	5
Author's Introduction	9
Highrise	15
Flowers	17
Little prince	19
Ode to a perforated styrofoam ceiling	21
Entrepreneur	22
The city speaks	24
Straight to the top	25
Knowledge fruit	26
In the elevator	28
Assembly line at the factory school	29
Searching	30
Lovers of the lonely	31
Where the path leads	32
Head in the cloud	33
Auction	34
Mine is bigger	38
Drops in the digital sea	39
Unmedicated	40
Urban no subs	42
The green	44
My local	46
Tales between tower blocks	49
Frazzled lines	50
Contagious	52
Remember	53
Within the noise	55
Author's notes on the poems	57
Advance comments	65

Please Stand Back From The Platform Door

HIGHRISE

By degrees over time I was built,
A foundation set by circumstance of birth,
And genetic roulette.

The view was great as a kid,
Before they put the walls in,
A façade slowly erected.
Fitting the architecture of the age,
The style of the city, mimicking the rest,
Another cloned building,
Built for doctors, lawyers and men,
Always aiming to be taller,
To wear the billboards of successful corporations,
Glass windows and cold air-conditioned interiors,

While the yells and laughter
Chiselled and reshaped the structure.

One day I demanded the windows be opened,
The view became more than a distant horizon:
I wanted more.
I smashed my own glass,
Graffitied walls when no one was looking,
Found holes and hidden vents,
Explored the nooks and crannies,
And found the piping underneath,
My own wiring,
My own electricity.

Tall enough, roof set,
Paying for overheads,
I realized that even if I could not change the foundation,
The faulty supports, crossed wires,
I would tear down my old walls,
Rebuild something of my own.

With just a hammer and a chisel,
No instructions to follow,
I knocked holes to let the light in,
Filled the insides with art.

Replaced the safety of fire escapes,
With love, risking to burn,
For the sake of something warm.

A building built with constructive habits,
Perhaps not as shiny as once envisioned,
One that does not fit the skyline.

But mine,
Ever mine.

A soaring tower
Reflecting a clear blue sky
Upon its open windows.

FLOWERS

They wrote about flowers.

We were taught in school,
A house is a square, two crosses for windows.
Triangle for a roof.
They never attached the price: a lifetime of labour,
For the unattainable.

They wrote about flowers.
But I know FANCL, I know Maxims,
Starbucks and McDonalds.
I know the rainbow sheen of polluted water,
About stay off the grass and
Speed walking through tourists.

They taught me very little about my own nature,
Those pale people from those far away islands
That we were told to listen to as children.

Tell me of the bamboo scaffolded towers;
Where the bamboo comes from.
The life cycles of self-taught graphic designers,
The ecosystem of concrete-paved, suit-wearing bankers,
Idealistic students and ignored beggars.

Or how to do tax returns.

I know about roses.
I've never seen a violet,

I know about love bought in malls;
Screen sold and soldered.
They taught me about another island in school.

They pretended truth.

They said: "This is English, this is Hong Kong."

And left us confused,
Between silencing our own words and wondering
Why there was nothing about us in any of the books.

LITTLE PRINCE

On Saturday I see a bald, white-skinned passenger of a car,
Turning a pointless wheel,
With a license plate that says
Snuggle Bug.

Travelling whole inches down the carpeted corridor,
Feet dangling uselessly,
Duck printed socks occasionally deigning to touch the ground.

Above

Steady hands, brown skinned, a lined face,
Hunched over the yellow roof, palms placed,
She pushes,
I risk a smile she does not return as she inches
The young prince down his road.

"Turn 'oun," garbles the prince
In a practiced way;
She obeys.

Turning in sync, to tiny hands, a tiny wheel,
Like a bridled mount over his roof,
I avoid the hunch of her head,
Notice,
How they inch
Their way back.

Above

Might have been his parents,
In a tower, on a plane,
Or perhaps at the pool, at tea, at lunch, working hard to afford
The Mid-Levels rent.

How they were missing out on this jewel
Of child's play

On Saturday,

I see her turn around again,
At the end of the corridor.

There must be an excuse for this epidemic,
A consistent tragedy of absent parents.
For multi-coloured Saturday children,
With their brown servants, forced to play.
Some of them smile,
Whilst with a contract their parents train
Their children to be at ease with absence,
Of parents, and servants.

On Saturday,

I see a bald, white-skinned passenger of a car,
Turning a pointless wheel,
With a license plate that read—

I turn around to avoid it.

ODE TO A PERFORATED STYROFOAM CEILING

Oh, perforated styrofoam ceiling!
How I lie upon this table,
Gaze up and wonder about ye!
The boss has gone to lunch, the office has emptied out:
I stayed in to finish entering data,
Then indulged in the freedom to lie down on this table.

How rare, how perfect an opportunity,
To gaze up at ye!

Oh perforated ceiling, thy holes they make me wonder,
I see pentagrams and constellations, star-speckled in the hundreds.
Big and small, thou styrofoam square framed by man-made metal,
Within a picture of some parallel universe's starry, starry night.

Oh, perforated ceiling! What forces shaped thy soul?
Was it the result of natural chemistry?
Or did thy creator thus compose;
Taking a needlepoint, a fountain pen, poking holes,
Creating constellations for my eyes to behold?
Did a creator smile with pride, creating gods and shapes,
Dot-drawn legends and imagined lines to render mouths agape!

I lie upon this table avoiding any screens.
For another forty-three minutes.
Whereupon I will return to my assigned task.

I make shapes upon the square,
Just one square among hundreds,
Whilst the office stays empty, and time ticks on regardless.

These shapes are my own,
Easily forgotten,

While the others are at lunch,
Hundreds among thousands.

ENTREPRENEUR

I'm going to develop an app
Tomorrow.

I'll borrow a developer account,
Lay my business plan out
In a PowerPoint presentation,
An investor demonstration,
As I invent something to finally
Stand out from the crowd.

The app will ping a notification,
When an idea is worth writing down
Mid-conversation,
Reminding us that this is the stuff of life,
Put life on pause and thumb tap the words out.

Like an idea Instagram—
Ideagram, it's a working title now.
The app will buzz
When a photo should be taken, let you know
To hurry before you miss the moment.

It'll keep track of when to keep your head down,
When to meet a stranger's gaze.
They'll be a way to rate the day,
The hours just passed,
The AI will learn the value of your time,
Capture misplaced lines,
That wander through your mind,
Compile inspiration, every original rhyme.

There will be a premium package.
A VIP programme,
With personalised customer support.
To tell you in advance if a day is meant to count,
Distinguish between humdrum and once-in-a-lifetime.
The app will tell you when you need to open your eyes,
So you can spend the rest of it sleepwalking.

It'll tell you when things matter.
When to carpe that diem,
Sift profundity from prattle,
An app,
For the demands of regret.

I'll build it,
Tomorrow.

Once I write down this idea,
Before I forget.

THE CITY SPEAKS

The Fear says: I saw you in the Admiralty platform door,
Three minutes staring at that dark mirror.
Give me the timespan of *please stand back*
To remind you, whip-fast
That you need to lose weight,
You fat fuck.
You're lazy, can't decide
Between the KitKat I test you with,
And paying for that Pure Membership.

You got to buy the right toys,
Stand straight, smile,
Get those Asia Miles,
Got news for you each morning,
Get sad, scared and angry all at once.
I got you a Netflix account for when it gets too much,
Dopamine fix for the rest of time,
Come home from work,
Shh,
I got stories, I got drinks, I got games,

Wake up asshat.

I've got a gun cocked and aimed,

Remember, when in doubt, it's your fault.
And don't forget to remind everyone else.

But when the ads are asleep,
During the rush-hour pause.
I hear a violin, a busker, a song.
I hear the sound of a skull bouncing off the floor.
I hear the eyes that shine quieter than the city lights.
Amidst the lies I hear the battle cry.

STRAIGHT TO THE TOP

The consonants on the subway walls are unravelling,
From letters to meaningless lines,
I try to ignore them, but I'm surfacing
In Admiralty, and the suited businessmen are black bags
Threatening to hood my eyes;
They say, get inside, your body should fit,
They wanna black bag my head.
Feel the explosion of questions in my gut,
As the ads become flashbangs of distractions
Where each ad cuts
From one scene of success

To another one;
In the ads they always zoom in on the jewelry,
I wanna wear someone who is wearing them,
I wanna make others feel bad at parties,
I wanna finally be the warden.

The skyscrapers demand I enter,
Look straight down; window faces a wall,
How small I looked
From up there—
How small I must look to everyone here.
Every day the fear breeds proofs,
Attaching price tags to dreams I auction off,
There's a ticker telling me to sell my stock,
I peddle busyness to acquaintances—
I am a rocket forever waiting to take off.

But I learned before I was ten—led by the hand,
That we live in a meritocracy,
So all the suicides must be wrong.

That the buildings just whispered to them:
Get off.

KNOWLEDGE FRUIT

Before the flood of words in virtual worlds,
Did we live in blissful ignorance?
Two by two in villages,
Marching to the same beat,
Before the noise online,
The all caps screams,
The vicious memes that cut,
Like mockery does,
When aimed right or left.

We walked in gardens, without headphones,
Listened to the silence, hands-free,
Believed in an angel with a flaming sword,
Who protected the gates,
Now we can all leave
Our minds via our eyes,
To bounce off satellites.

Very Apple,
The fruit of knowledge.
We take bites,
In those vast, empty Apple stores,
It's something to do with snakes,
And a book, written in Greek.
I could look it up on my IPhone.
Samsung a galaxy into existence.
Tablets, from chiselled stone to etched wax,
To touch screen memory palimpsest.

Reach out and speak, finger and thumb
On plastic, emote, these oceans are not enough,
We've built electric highways between our islands.
Speed of light, faster than thought—

We live in such great times, so much everything,
We have everything today,
In this now,
In this moment,
In these perpetual revelations, conclusions,
Revolutions.

A billion pages telling us how to be human.

IN THE ELEVATOR

It is in our bones
To speak to each other up close.

Thank Jobs for smartphones,
So our eyes have somewhere to go,

And rest, forced to press against each other
In the elevator on the way to work.

Even enforced physical contact
Is not enough to make us care.

I'm glad there is so much porn
To satisfy the need to touch and feel

In the dignified silence of our rooms,
Piping voices in our ears with headphones.

Texting is a triumph: now, our villages
Follow us in our pockets,

Snapshots manicured on screen,
Frozen words, life on pause, propped up memories—

We have made elevators,
That now feel awkward:

We have conquered our humanity
Despite so little space.

We have made loneliness a disease.

ASSEMBLY LINE AT THE FACTORY SCHOOL

Another morning.
Attempt to return to dreams of sex and freedom.
Fifteen more minutes warden,
I'm sure I'll find happiness before then.

Another morning.
Programming kicks in:
I am an operating system
Booting through showers, cereal; such efficient boxed up calories;
Coffee ahhhhhh
                    I'll wake up someday.

Speed walk to the transport.
Hang head disappointed.
Look defeated on the MTR;
Defeated by employment:
I am a tool employed,
I am contributing,
Not sure where, but the energy I'm generating—
Money's like energy it makes the economy
Do things.

When the bell rings take a moment to
Assume the smile; put on your eyes.
Swallow the regurgitated dreams.
The clock's your salvation,
Play the game where you look away then
Look back after forty-two minutes.
Heaven's only a Friday away.

There's a child whose eyes still have the fire,
                              They are tearing up the rules.

A part of me is proud.
The other holds the whip.

SEARCHING

We live in the age of everything.
For every question, a googleplex of answers,
Even if we don't actually look for them.

Turn to our phones, thumb it into existence,
No need to wait,
We read, learn, and sate:
The mystery is answered.

What was it like before?
To not know,
To be certain you cannot know.

Simpler language,
Simple WikiHow ELI5 Quora
Yahoo Questions and Answers
And listicles and 'best ofs'
TL; DR—
I carry both a library and an amusement park.

LOVERS OF THE LONELY

In the morning you are a distant face,
Someone who laughed at all my jokes,
Something to hold.

If I close my eyes tight,
Smother my ears with a pillow,
I can almost remember what you felt like.

Your name is a secret word,
Opening doors in my head,
But I can't go back to where we met.
I remember being happy; white light, bright eyes.

While the sun is up I sometimes dream eyes open,
Drifting through trains and buses, under faded skies.

I dream that you are asleep, somewhere else in this world,
Sending yourself to the place we met, and I bring you the same
Sad comfort you gave me. Till we both wake,
And drown in our days.

WHERE THE PATH LEADS

The sun hung like a
Glowing orange lamp, behind
A gauze of orange smog.
Its light as sickly as cyclones of
Stage lighting smoke.

In the park, the toy dogs are
Held down for photo-shoots,
As tourists take photos of owners taking photos.

The grey marred canvas
Outlines the city scratching sky, as
Boats trundle by on a sea that ripples
Whip-cracked fabric,
Peaks and troughs grasping across a satin sheet.

We walk on concrete, call it a park,
The grey imitation of a forest long gone.
The scooters twist and
Turn past,
As children swerve around adults,
Children ticking their way to adulthood,

Time ticks by.
A minute hand, jagged,
Stuttering forwards, as cells die, copy
With minuscule errors,
Somewhere in our systems,
As we lap the park,
Onwards into habit,
And the smiles fill the space in time.

While the glass forest reflects
Vague silhouettes, dulled by the haze that drifts in the air,
In the rattling hills of the skyline,
A sketch of progress.

HEAD IN THE CLOUD

What was it like,
When we didn't have someone,
Waiting for us all the time?

To respond, to like, to read,
A friend, an idol, a deity,
All of these people,
Waiting for an answer.

Was it more lonely?

What was it like?
When there wasn't someone better around,
Manifold Gods, in creative pantheons,
Billion strong typists, now watch us, or do you watch them?
Watch their stories, their art, their insta better Instagram.

What was it like when we weren't always trying to create?
When Vincent Van Goh couldn't wink at your painting.

What was it like?
When we didn't know how many people died?

There are so many front pages,
Where's the frontest?
We would need compound eyes,
Like these glassed over skyscrapers,
This progress, these satellites.
To see it all, what was it like?

I can't remember;
My memory's on my hard drive,
I mean my USB; I mean
It's in the cloud,
My memories are in the cloud.
It floats forward, I think.

AUCTION

Good evening ladies and gentlemen.

I will now begin the primary auction,
Followed by a secondary auction after I leave
In which we will sell tangible goods.

I will be auctioning off abstract concepts,
Which cannot be bought with money.
Thus for the purposes of Hong Kong,
It is arguable that these items are effectively worthless,
But we will pretend that we can buy property with them,
Or at least mental real estate, if it helps.

For our first item we will have...

An amateur undiscovered artist,
A writer of undiscovered literature
Currently drowning in a sea coloured fifty shades of Gray...
We will start the bidding at,
One reader per word,
One reader per word?
Can I get a blog with good traffic,
One blog with good traffic?

Going once...

Going twice…

SOLD
Back to the writer of undiscovered literature.
Write more old man, we'll get back to you in a year.

For our second item we have…

A speech from your favorite poet,
That's right, ladies and gentlemen,
That asinine line you memorised,
The one you whisper to yourself on the john,
On a bad day, the desktop wallpaper,

The poet's going to visit, you get to say:
"You saved my life."
We will start the bidding at—
One honest poem for a favourite fan,
Can I get one honest poem for a favourite fan?
No?

Going once...

Going twice...

Sold to the silent majority of Hong Kong.

Can I get a kid who'd rather not be a banker,
A doctor, or
God forbid...a lawyer?
Can I get a kid who is stupid enough to make stories?
Can I get a kid in this city
Who isn't ten feet from a building's edge?
No.
Fine.
After all, how are we going to live?
Words don't pay the rent.

Let's carry on.

For our crowning item, we will have a prophecy
Ladies and gentlemen,
A science-fiction prophecy about global warming
Ladies and gentlemen,
A plastic nation on the Pacific Ocean,
One speech to change one heart to change one family to change one world,
We will start the bidding at,
No hope,
No hope ladies gentlemen,
Lies, so many lies, ladies and gentlemen,
We will start the bidding at two dinners at Petrus
Discussing the imminent housing bubble ladies and gentlemen,
We will start the bidding at Hublot ladies and gentlemen,
We will start with some fool with a dream and a pen

Alone at their desk, ladies and gentlemen,
We will start with the truth.

Can I get two plastic bags, ladies and gentlemen?
Can I get cover from the rain, ladies and gentlemen?
Can I get hope, ladies and gentlemen?

Going once...

Going twice...

Going three times...

Going twenty. Going fifty....

Going as long as we can go, in theory.

Going the inalienable rights,
Going equality,
Going the young.

Going the artists who still paint with every colour,
Going the Davids in the face of Goliaths.

Going the dreamers.

Unsold.

Because we will not yet sell our home just yet,
For an annual GDP growth of 6.7%,

Finally...

We have here a nano-pen by Mont Blanc,
Never to be used for anything except signatures, ladies and gentlemen,
A single signature to change 10,000 jobs, ladies and gentlemen,
A single signature to move millions of dollars, ladies and gentlemen,
A single signature to sit in a desk, ladies and gentlemen.

I will start the bidding at the first and the last word,

Can I get someone to remember the importance of stories, ladies and gentlemen,
Can I get some honesty ladies and gentlemen,

Going once…

Going twice...

SOLD
To the writers,
Every foolish, hopeful, necessary one of them.

Item zero: here is our home,
One of a kind,
Limited production,
Owned by no one.

Can I get the writers who try to remind us, ladies and gentlemen,
Can I get the future, ladies and gentlemen,
Can I get the future, ladies and gentlemen,
Can I get humans, ladies and gentlemen?

Can I get you?

Ladies and gentlemen.

Going once…

Going twice...

MINE IS BIGGER

Arise, glossy erections;
Steely-eyed bird cages,
Edifices that hurl themselves
Towards the sky.

Glass bricks,
Structural physics,
A premature eruption
That fills the air

Amidst the rising plumes of
Skyscraping affection
Their heads emerge,
These empty ejections

Like discarded cases
Of some shrunken rockets.

DROPS IN THE DIGITAL SEA

Michelangelo emailed me his David.
He's painting on Photoshop,
But the bitmap began to rot:
I don't have the heart to tell him
That they are lingering on a hard drive
Tens of thousands of minutes too old,
In the steady evolution of USB slots and wireless thoughts
That leaves his wire trailing behind.

Chuck Berry played once in a tiny club,
Paid in drinks, before the cover bands went on.
He tries Spotify, but can't comprehend the new age,
So old he still plays Guitar Hero.
On YouTube he's got ten subs, his view count's from his friends.,
He's decided his dreams aren't Kanye enough,
They're lost in a new kind of expanding ocean.

Dostoyevsky tried to tweet an agent his blurb,
But he kept violating the character limit,
He's drowning in compressed fan fiction,
Leonardo thinks there's nothing left to invent,
There's a listicle of newer inventions.

He opens the page every morning,
Drinking the ocean because it's too big to dream in.

UNMEDICATED

They tell me I'm sick
'Cause in the mornings I wanna lie back down;
Too sick to get up and go to work;
So sick I wanna scream at the city
Drown out the pile-drivers, the horns,
The *let's do lunches* and
Favours recorded on Gmail calendars,

I'm so sick, my eyes are seeing tumours,
My ears are hearing torture,
This tongue wants to spit the steel from its pores—

I need my pills.

I can't breathe and they all want to connect
Let's touch base, they say
And my head says it's lies;
My nose is smelling bullshit,
Gallons and gallons of concrete occluded sewage,

There's mansions where every square foot
Is worth more than someone else's family.
We put price tags on everything,
They keep wanting to connect,
But my sickness—

There's a Ferrari crawling through traffic,
A chariot on parade, a taipan on his triumph,
Spotify is playing on his iPhone,
No one is whispering in his ear
You're not a God.
He's chosen a track that says he's badass,
Says he's money,
Says he's free and he made it;
Caesar's just a salad; he eats it—

But these folks are listening to tracks
That teamed up with car window glass
To cover up the Cantonese yells of construction workers.
They build empty office lobbies big as ancient palaces,
Reflecting prisons in their marble floor—

But I'm fucking crazy, right?

The guy's staring at his phone, cursing when he has to swerve,
Because a sixty-year-old grandma is pushing a trolley full of trash,
Cheaper than the steak he bought from Citysuper
'Cause he's a superman,
'Cause this city's super, man
And I'm moving super fast—

If I take enough pills—
        I can't think too much—
                Of how little, how wrong, how sick we all are—

How ill this place is.

They want to connect.
They want to share.
I want to grab them by the hair and yell,
What have we done?

Stop texting me and look,
Look—

Okay I took
My pills.

I'll be fine by tomorrow—
                I'll be quiet again, tomorrow—
                                and I'll go back to work—

URBAN NO SUBS

I didn't know I was allowed to be angry that I didn't have a voice.
I remember that.

I remember being made to feel guilty for who I was;
It makes me realise how many people still are.

I don't like the poems that excise mobile phones,
The internet;
Like we're still living in the fields.

The biggest field I've seen is Victoria Park,
And it's just dirt and grass.

These pastoral poems trim away the actual life,
Leave behind
The leavings of other poems from other times,

Rather than look outside
Buried in books, bent-forward
Folded-over, peering into their own navel.

They transported their houses to our city.
They call it Plantation Road
Because the British brought back their own trees,
Planted the seeds so they could cover up the tropical, tiger-
spawning jungle.

How many stories begin with descriptions of the insides of
suburban homes?
I've never known sub, just urban.
This city is a window into the future;
We're a trailer of what's to come.

I can't find five novels about growing up in Pok Fu Lam,
Watching Cyberport metastasize over the years;
They skip to being mesmerized by wet markets and dim sum.

I want to read about underage flights to Lan Kwai Fong,
Cafés obliterated for more apparel stores,
Punjabis on scooters swerving through traffic,
Open mic buskers trying to make it,
Taxi drivers juggling four phones for rent—

But I don't want to write about them.
It's scary trying to speak about something others haven't spoken of yet,
It's hard to tell whether it makes any sense.

THE GREEN

I've been seeing therapists, psychiatrists, self-advisists,
YouTubers, advice-givers and gods for long enough,
That I could take the needle and plunge it, right into my skull,
Right where the Green is.

I do it in the mirror, at a restroom in Starbucks.
Pull on the plunger, watch the acid coming out.
It's dark lime, translucent with flakes.
Some neurons as well, but it's worth it.

I thwack the needle with a finger flick,
The juice churns a bit, it's so dirty.
I feel okay, I feel good, I feel perfectly empty.

Give the needle a sniff,
Smells like iron and batteries,
Strong as bad wine and rust,
Like the rot of childhood,
When the teachers syringed the Green into my mouth,
Even if I choked,
It was for my own good;
It was medicine,
A vaccine for failure, humiliation, divergence—
I want to sell the runoff.

Maybe I can produce more,
Weekly, daily, syringing it off,
But where to sell it?

I'll try Craigslist.

Perfect for people you want to completely fuck up.
Pick your CEO, spike his Nespresso.
The Green will breed fears over the months,
They'll doubt themselves, then stop coming to work,
Their self-esteem obliterated.

If you weaponise it, in aerosol form,
You could spray it over entire cities,
Watch over years how the sensitive ones kill themselves,
Watch the homogeneity set, watch them wreck their planet.

I press the syringe to my cheek: it feels cold.
I feel like I can't relate to anyone else in this Starbucks.
But I want to talk, to connect to them—that's crazy,
They are strangers—maybe one tiny taste
Of the Green, before I'm too infected—

It was a vaccine all along.

What have I done?
I'm failing at my job.

I must work hard to get promoted,
Put drops of the Green into my minions' mugs,
They hang onto my words, so it'll spread through touch,
Start a family and feed them the drug,
Daddy's acid, while they are young.
Put it in movies, sell it in shops,
Till everyone is breathing it in and out.
Keep sharing the needle,
It'll spread quicker this way.
It's only a pinch,
Protecting us from the real pain.

I leave a bit of it in my head,
So I don't change my mind too often

MY LOCAL

An expat and me,
We speak the same speak.
But I get it, I don't look Chinese.

We sound the same.
Which means what, exactly?
It's hard to explain so—
        America sure, California yeah,
        Canada if you like, British fine.

What did your mum tell you never to buy
In 7/11?
Pork floss and pork sticks,
I liked cuttlefish, it's basically chewing gum,
Begged for blue Kinder surprise from Wellcome—
        Sure, let's talk about Donald Trump.
        What a jerk, right?

I miss that food court in Pacific Place sometimes.
You know the one before Swire dressed it up,
The one with KFC and Pizza Hut,
Checked out new releases with girls in Hong Kong Records
And at night, went to Hong Kong park.
Then they built the IFC, with free public space!—
        Oh, you went to the pub?
        That's cool.
        Me too, yeah, all the bars,

Would have drunk in them in a parallel world if I had been
A white boy from DB at 15.
But I liked the LAN cafés really,
Aztec and Arcades in Causeway Bay,
Cheap siu mai and cup noodles for days.
Wanchai computer malls, Southorn Playground talking smack,
At Game Empire the lady spoke English, how about that!—
        That's right, that's all I speak...
        Yeah, I should learn Cantonese.
        That's great, good pronunciation.
        I think.

Remember Freddy saying it's gonna rain?
AWWW or OOOO
Remember praying for Black Rainstorm or T8?
We had ATV, TVB, World and Pearl (not Jade)
At 6:30pm, *The following broadcast will be in Putonghua.*
Ocean Park's a long drive—well not anymore,
Remember the shark tunnel?
The Jumbo Restaurant everyone knew had terrible food,
Lockhart Road dives.
Carnegie's, ten-dollar shot Wednesdays—
    Oh not anymore? Swindler's Gone?
    Not Neptune of course.

Wanna Sing K?
Play dice at Barn 2? Before it moved.
Remember when the Star Ferry had rickshaws?
Remember SARS and Bird Flu?

The difference between us:
I'm excellent at pretending to be you.

I grew up on charsiu,
My city's strange, speaks a different language,
But I'm used to it, it's why I never learned,
Because home and truth is a grey fuzzy line,
You won't find it on the MTR.
Looks Eurasian sometimes,
Or third-generation, Sindhi diamond trader-like,
Filipino musicians hustling past midnight.
FANCL ads that change, but one of the few companies who keep
Less Is More for two decades.
Our version of Goddesses:
Like the voice on the MTR,
Like Anson Chan whenever she shows up,

Remember how we didn't go to parks?
Scab your knees on concrete,
Never touch the grass.

I like to say,
I'm from somewhere else, third culture kid, international.
But that's bullshit somedays.
I'm from Hong Kong.
This multi-coloured seven million strong city,
That honestly,
You don't know that much about.
And neither do I.
That's the point. It's too big.

Because Hong Kong's not the city of light—
It's the city of change,
Always moving, nothing lasts, especially the ads.
Even the coast, the lines, the land.

Remember those months when we could sit cross-legged
on Des Voeux Road?
Remember hearing that anthem, that Canto song, by Beyond?

Does anyone know the chorus?

And in a few years, the next expats will come,
They'll never get how important those candlelight vigils were.
This place we grew up in,
We love it to death.

This is my home.

I was half-raised by Filipinos,
Branded goods, learning the difference between Fake and Cheap,
Watching it all change.

But yeah,
I get what you're saying

I should learn Cantonese,
So I can finally understand what all the locals mean.

TALES BETWEEN TOWER BLOCKS

Were all the lights to come undone
Before midnight arrived,
Detaching like paper sheets from the high-rise stories,
We would watch the crowds continue unabated.

They'd cut through the paper with scissor legs
They'd push them aside to get a better look at
The ad covered walls.
No space left,
For your words except,

When stretched,

As wide a sheet as the city is broad.
Pin it down like a circus tent held in place,
By sleeping buses in midnight bus stations,
By the climbing bamboo and the smothered aspirations,
Poke holes in the paper for the lonely to breathe.

Juggle rejected tales, poems, plays,
Clown your way above the crowds on the highest stilts.
Deposit the unfinished in the tipping jars of moth-life cafés.

Write on anyway.

Tell one story, among the millions,
That never comes undone.

FRAZZLED LINES

Is everyone in the carriage faking their smiles?
It can't be:
See the parent. Couple. Child.
See the phone-worship.
Does anyone else want to hit the emergency stop?
There must be others in this car,
I want the PA to announce,
That the lines do not work anymore.
They do not work for the frazzled.

My phone offers something, I forget,
But if I check,
I can check at the speed of thought.
Somebody will say something,
Some Facebook friend, some news, an update,
There is a river of noise.
But these frazzled lines won't twist back
To silence, twist back to habit.
The fear is in the train,
This snake steel gullet.

But I made a bookmark last time I sat,

And thought about it all.

I championed my way through my keyboard,
Through bedroom 1AM week-morning fear
To the places where the frazzled lines meet,

They speak on forums,
In tweets.
They have a subreddit,
Where held hands look like two lines of comments,
And smiles are an upvoted promise,
With kind chatroom respite offers,
Sermons given by part-time prophets,
As full-time bloggers confess,
The lines meet in comment boxes,
And private messages.

The lines from my frazzled head,
To my shaking hand,
Through my cracked screen,
To the other non-smilers,
On all the other trains.

We still keep Gods as statues,
But these places you cannot stand in,
Cannot walk in or touch,
Are our online churches, perhaps cathedral enough,
To find the lost for a time,
To meet at the end of the frazzled lines.

CONTAGIOUS

Have you ever caught a smile?

A smile pitched across the pavement.

Never asked for,

A smile that infected your face,

Curved around the runoff of plastic mountains,
Black and sagging, they spew open like glaciers
Melting, excavating empty packaging,
Broken glass graveyards tinkle like a holiday underfoot,
Crushed by marching office-black shoes,
Habits safe as phones, under a sky too orange,
Blues before the weekend,
While the frowns collect like slumped cigarettes,
Close to the pavement, squashed to silence on the train,
Another door for another meal for another day,

Till the supermarkets dim the lights, the food disappears off-stage,
The water buckets in alleyways, closed kitchens with oil stains,
The night cleaners, and night insects, go to streets, to clean away,

But I caught a smile on the train.

Pressed through the plastic, the speed-walking and smog;
This space between us was not what I was taught.

This space that can be crossed.

REMEMBER

Minibus ride,
Leafy slope veil,
Gaps between reveal
The green revelation of a valley.
The empty air that hangs between hills.

These empty spaces
Take my breath,
Pull it from my lungs,
Bid me to follow it.
Back to an ancestral home.

On plains,
A Serengeti past.
Is there a part of me that leaps
At solitary trees?
Did we smile?
Did we laugh and cry?
Between fighting for what we thought of,
And still think of, as ours.

Did the green mean peace for weary eyes?

I sit inside concrete cubes,
Get lost in a crowd of stories,
Climb with only my feet.
Soar and rise and dive,
Inside steel beasts.

Does the blue, the green
Set hearts to rest?
Did any part of us not leap

At all these empty spaces?

Filled with life,
With trees,
Crystal strands of streams.

Before we brought the floods
That rose to drown our seeds
Before the whips.

I would not want to return to it.
I just wonder
What it felt like to be that free.

WITHIN THE NOISE

The pile-drivers and power-drills chiselled out a hole
That time then filled with peace and quiet. The crowds
Of Causeway Bay marched in daytime riot, 'til
They dug through time and open space where I could
Sit and notice silence.

The frantic pain in my stomach, tendons I ripped
And bones I broke, healed till they birthed a new
Body, born again, free from pain, I took note of
Noises that painted my hours, clamouring
Like a hell-sent chorus.

On some mornings, on hard-won happy days,
I have trained my ears to listen to silence
And hear the music in-between the noises,
Not ringing, not tinnitus
But joy.

AUTHOR'S NOTES ON THE POEMS

The pace of change in Hong Kong is rapid. Descriptions and comments are accurate at the time of final editing (October 2021).

FLOWERS

School: I was raised in Hong Kong in a school (part of the group of schools in the English Schools Foundation (ESF), which followed the British school system), and was taught primarily by British teachers.
"FANCL": Popular cosmetic company in Hong Kong, especially known for their skin-whitening products and their eternal slogan: Less is More.
Maxims: A franchise of local eateries, one of the biggest in Hong Kong.
Bamboo-scaffolded towers: In Hong Kong, scaffolding is made with bamboo, due to its high tensile strength.

LITTLE PRINCE

Brown-skinned / brown servants: A reference to a domestic helper in Hong Kong. Most often ethnically from South East Asia or the Philippines. These migrant workers make up 370,000 people in Hong Kong, as live-in staff, often under poor conditions, working long hours, for a low wage by Hong Kong standards. They are expected to be nannies, cleaners, and cooks.
The prince: in Cantonese, "little prince" is pejorative for a spoiled young boy in a family.
Mid Levels Rent: Mid-Levels is an expensive and prestigious residential area on Hong Kong island.

ODE TO A PERFORATED STYROFOAM CEILING

Hundreds among thousands: During lunchtime, the vast majority of workers in Hong Kong eat lunch outside, going to restaurants and the like.

ENTREPRENEUR

App: Program on a phone.
Instagram: Popular photo-sharing app where people can share their own personal stories and images.
PowerPoint: Slideshow presentation program often used in corporate settings.
Carpe that Diem: Carpe Diem—Latin for "seize the day".

THE CITY SPEAKS

KitKat: Popular chocolate bar in Hong Kong.
Pure Membership: "Pure" is a brand of expensive gyms in Hong Kong.
Asia Miles: A frequent-flyer rewards program used by the largest Asian airlines.
Netflix: Popular subscription-based video streaming app.
Dopamine fix: A neurochemical associated with reward and pleasure in the brain.

STRAIGHT TO THE TOP

Admiralty: A subway station hub in Hong Kong where many lines converge.

KNOWLEDGE FRUIT

All caps screams: Writing in all capitals, usually thought of as shouting or screaming online.
Apple: Multinational company that invented the smartphone / creates Apple technology products.
Apple stores: Usually very spacious and prestigious, Apple stores are known for their minimalist design.

IN THE ELEVATOR

Jobs for smartphones: Reference to Steve Jobs, inventor of the Iphone.

ASSEMBLY LINE AT THE FACTORY SCHOOL

MTR: Mass transit railway, Hong Kong's subway system.

SEARCHING

Wikihow: Reference to the website www.wikihow.com/, a site that explains how things work.

ELI5: "Explain like I am 5", a popular concept online where a complex thing is explained simply to someone, preferably at the level of a five year old.

Quora: a reference to the website www.quora.com, where questions are asked and answered by voted-on experts.

Yahoo Questions and Answers: A reference to the website answers.yahoo.com/, where questions are asked and answered by members on any topic.

Listicles: Articles that are primarily lists, like "top 10 ways to…" etc.

"Best ofs": Online compilations of the 'best' posts on a website, curated or voted as such by others.

TL; DR: "Too long, didn't read", an abbreviation put at the end of a long post that either summarizes the post (a one or two sentence summary of the article) or is used pejoratively to suggest a post is too long. Also implies one cannot be bothered to read the whole article and would prefer a simplified version.

HEAD IN THE CLOUD

Instagram: Popular photo-sharing app where people can share their own personal stories and images.

Cloud: The general term for storing information online, rather than saving it locally to your computer, such as through using Google documents or ICloud

Hard drive: Where information is stored long-term on a computer.

USB: Short form for a memory stick used to store information externally.

AUCTION

Fifty Shades Of Gray: Hugely popular light erotic novel, popularly considered to be terribly written.

Desktop wallpaper: Background image of the default screen of your computer.

Petrus: Extremely expensive famous French restaurant in Hong Kong.

Hublot: Internationally recognized luxury watch brand.

Mont Blanc: Luxury pen brand.

DROPS IN THE DIGITAL SEA

Photoshop: Popular image-editing software.
Bitmap: Very old file format for images, not as popular these days.
Hard drive: Where information is stored long-term on a computer.
USB slot: Port where a memory stick plugs into a computer.
Spotify: Popular music playing/sharing app.
Guitar Hero: Video game from around 2005, no longer popular, where you played using a plastic guitar to mimic popular songs.
YouTube: Popular video sharing website.
Kanye: Reference to international pop superstar and 2020 presidential candidate Kanye West.
Tweet: Reference to Twitter, where posts are limited to 280 characters.
Compressed Fanfiction: Compressed is a reference to file. compression, where a programme is used to shrink down the size of a file. Fanfiction is the genre of amateur writers writing spin-off stories of famous characters in popular novels.
Listicle: Articles that are primarily lists, like "top 10 inventions…" etc.

UNMEDICATED

Let's touch base: An idiom often seen in business contexts meaning to make contact or reconnect with someone briefly, such as in "let's touch base next week."
Taipan: In the nineteenth and early twentieth centuries, taipans were foreign-born businessmen who headed large Hong trading houses such as Jardine, Matheson & Co., Swire, and Dent & Co. amongst others. Literally "top-class" it now refers to a senior business executive or entrepreneur operating in China or Hong Kong.
Triumph: Reference to the ancient Roman tradition which celebrated a returning conqueror with a parade, notably Julius Caesar after his campaign in Gaul.
Citysuper: Upmarket supermarket chain.

URBAN NO SUBS

Victoria Park: Park in the centre of the city.
Plantation Road: Exceedingly expensive residential area. Located on The Peak, it is one of Hong Kong's most exclusive addresses, and where, in early days before air-conditioning, senior colonial

government officials summered due to its cooler microclimate.
Pok Fu Lam: Residential area on the south side of the city.
Cyberport: 'Tech hub' office and retail complex with a reputation as a 'ghost town', mostly developed in Pok Fu Lam between 2002 and 2008.

THE GREEN

Craigslist: An online personal ads platform with a reputation for underhanded deals and scams.
Nespresso: High-end coffee capsule brand manufacturer.

MY LOCAL

7/11: Ubiquitous twenty-four hour convenience store.
Pork floss, pork sticks, cuttlefish: Local packaged snacks inundated with preservatives.
Wellcome: Supermarket chain.
Blue Kinder Surprise: Chocolate egg with a toy inside, now discontinued for safety reasons. Those in blue were marketed towards boys, pink for girls.
Pacific Place: Shopping-mall in Admiralty.
Swire: One of the early British (Scottish) businesses in Hong Kong, now a major land-owner. Owns Pacific Place.
Hong Kong Records: Now extinct music store.
Hong Kong Park: Park adjacent to Pacific Place, in the heart of the city.
IFC: International Finance Center: Large office building with attached mall. There is an outdoor seating area available to the public on the top of the mall.
DB: Short for "Discovery Bay", a residential area on one of the outlying islands, known for having a large western, expat population.
LAN cafés: Also known as cybercafés, where you are charged by the hour to use their computers to play games on.
Aztec: Name of a LAN café chain in Hong Kong (now extinct).
Causeway Bay: Densely-populated shopping district on Hong Kong Island.
Siu mai: Popular form of dim sum, can be bought from street vendors and in convenience stores as well as restaurants.
Cup Noodles: Instant packaged noodles in a styrofoam cup.
Wanchai: Area on Hong Kong island, known for its red-light district, government buildings, offices, and shops.

Wanchai computer malls: A shopping market for computer parts, games, peripherals and assorted tech.
Southorn Playground: A public area with basketball courts and football pitches in Wanchai, used by locals, surrounded by the city.
Game Empire: Name of a LAN cafe (now extinct).
Freddy: Animated character on the Hong Kong TV channel TVB Pearl. Appears at the end of weather reports along with the next day's weather and audio of either "OOOO" or "AWWW", depending on whether the forecast was for good or bad weather.
Black Rainstorm: A type of rainstorm signal publicly broadcast by the government during severe inclement weather. Schools are closed during black rainstorms.
T8: A type of typhoon signal when a severe typhoon hits Hong Kong. Schools and offices close during a T8 signal.
ATV, TVB, World and Pearl (not Jade): All are local Hong Kong TV channels that broadcast in English. TVB Jade broadcast in Cantonese.
The following broadcast will be in Putonghua: Voiceover at 6:30 pm on TVB Pearl before an hour of broadcast in Putonghua.
Ocean Park: Hong Kong's local amusement park and aquarium.
Jumbo Restaurant: Hong Kong's famous floating restaurant, visited mainly by tourists.
Lockhart Road dives: Located in Wanchai's red-light district. Mostly bars and unofficial brothels.
Carnegie's, ten-dollar shot Wednesdays: Bar on Lockhart Road, known for its shots for ten dollars on Wednesdays.
Swindler's: Bar on Lockhart Road (now extinct).
Neptune: Seedy bar that doubles as a place for prostitutes to meet potential customers.
Sing K: Local colloquialism for going to karaoke.
Barn 2: Bar visited almost entirely by locals.
Charsiu: Barbecue pork. Quintessential Hong Kong meat dish.
Star Ferry: Hong Kong's famous ferry that traverses Victoria Harbour.
SARS: Contagious and lethal virus pandemic in Hong Kong in 2002 - 2004.
Bird Flu: The outbreak of bird flu which occurred in 2008.
Eurasian: Term for people of mixed Asian and western descent.
Sindhi: Majority ethnic Indian group in Hong Kong.

"FANCL": As above, popular cosmetic company in Hong Kong, especially known for their skin whitening products and their eternal slogan: "Less is More".
Third culture kid(s): People raised in a culture other than their parents' or the culture of their country of nationality, and who also live in a different environment during a significant part of their child development years.

FRAZZLED LINES

Tweets: Reference to Twitter, where posts are limited to 280 characters.
Subreddits: Reference to reddit.com, where anyone can post on a variety of topics. Subreddits are specialized pages that focus on a certain topic, from sports teams to jokes to abstract concepts.
Upvote: System on Reddit for approving of, encouraging and liking specific posts and comments. The most popular ones rise to the top and become visible to everyone else.
Chatroom: Colloquialism for online forums for discussion.

REMEMBER

Minibus: Ubiquitous public transport in Hong Kong. Nineteen seats at max capacity.

WITHIN THE NOISE

Causeway Bay: Densely populated shopping district on Hong Kong Island.

ADVANCE COMMENTS

The MTR announcement in the title is an apt metaphor for Hong Kong, a city where the only constant is constant change. The persona/narrator in these poems sifts through the real and hyperreal to locate a HK identity (that is not mono-cultural) and memories (that are not stored on a hard drive). 'Flowers' points up the disparity between the lived experience of HK (brand names, bamboo scaffolding and bankers) and what gets taught in school. We are offered shifting perspectives on this city of façades (in both senses). Its busy-ness, its bigger-ness, instant response, instant gratification leaves little room for self-doubt. There is a rich tonal range here from mordant wit (an office worker who lies on a table to look up at "stars" in a perforated styrofoam ceiling) to darker moods where vertiginous glass skyscrapers whisper "get off" to would-be suicides. The collection is especially strong on our technology-mediated existences. 'Knowledge Fruit' conjures up a world of selfies, apps, chatrooms and not-so-smart phones, dead souls on the MTR who endure the daily Purgatory of their devices, when memes may morph to screams. The author is not Chinese, but he is emphatically a true local. The evocation of his city in these poems is authentic and affectionate (the last word of the collection is "joy")—a tour de force.

—Peter Kennedy
School of English,
University of Hong Kong

Almost a hundred years ago Fritz Lang's film *Metropolis* offered us a vision of the future and in Vishal Nanda's debut collection *Please Stand Back From The Platform Door* we have arrived there. But we can't be anywhere else other than Hong Kong in 2021 where "we have conquered humanity despite so little space" ('In the Elevator') with this "third culture kid" who "grew up on charsiu" ('My Local') and who, thanks to technology, carries "both a library and an amusement park" ('Searching') in his pocket but needs to be told "where the bamboo comes from" ('Flowers'). Through his poems we enter a live stream of this compulsively changing city of "glossy erections; steely-eyed bird cages" ('Mine is bigger') and "Styrofoam ceilings" ('Ode to a perforated Styrofoam ceiling'). Through his words we have a heartfelt contemplation of what it means to belong, to be angry, to struggle with and survive the modern demons that threaten our mental health: what it means to be human in Hong Kong right here, right now. Amid this clamour he asks, "can I get the future ladies and gentlemen?" ('Auction') and comes back with an emphatic takeaway message—"hear the music in between the noise. Not ringing, not tinnitus. But joy." ('Within the noise').

—Neil Douglas
London
October 2021

Vishal Nanda's wonderful panorama of Hong Kong offers the reader a kaleidoscope of memorable poetry. His *Please Stand Back from the Platform Door* is a cornucopia of evocative emotion—sometimes mirroring the author's anxiety and at other times his exuberance for the moment—a *joi de vivre*. Indeed, there is a visual playfulness in Nanda's words which will remain in the reader's mind for some time.

—J. P. Linstroth,
Proverse Prize 2019 (*Epochal Reckonings*)
Florida USA

Every writer needs a catalyst, or a judicious combination of trigger factors, to find the true, genuine 'voice' that resonates because it comes from deep within. Vishal has found his voice with this collection, and I know he will not stop here. I look forward to his continuing his literary journey, as he observes and describes the world around him in his own discerning way.

—David McMahon,
Author of *Vegemite Vindaloo*, Penguin India

As if a bright focus light is suddenly switched on, we see afresh the business of living in Vishal Nanda's highly perceptive and phenomenal mirroring of contemporary life:—the push button ease, the touch and feel starved existence where "loneliness" is "a disease" ('In the Elevator'), "villages / Follow us in our pockets" ('In the Elevator'), and "Heaven's only a Friday away" ('Assembly Line at the Factory School').

Nanda's slick turn of phrase and tongue in cheek panache swings between the irreverent and soulful. Definitely a book for the humans of today!

—Lily Swarn,

Internationally awarded, multilingual poet, author,
Peace and Humanity Ambassador, Waheed Centre for Humanity and Humanitarianism Development, Ghana

SOME POETRY AND POETRY COLLECTIONS
Published by Proverse Hong Kong

A Gateway Has Opened, by Liam Blackford. November 2021.

Alphabet, by Andrew S. Guthrie. 2015.

Astra and Sebastian, by L.W. Illsley. 2011.

Black Holes Within Us (translation from Macedonian), by Marta Markoska. 2021.

Bliss of Bewilderment, by Birgit Bunzel Linder. 2017.

The Burning Lake, by Jonathan Locke Hart. 2016.

Celestial Promise, by Hayley Ann Solomon. 2017.

Chasing light, by Patricia Glinton Meicholas. 2013.

China suite and other poems, by Gillian Bickley. 2009.

Epochal Reckonings, by J.P. Linstroth. 2020.

For the record and other poems of Hong Kong, by Gillian Bickley. 2003.

Frida Kahlo's cry and other poems, by Laura Solomon. 2015.

Grandfather's Robin, by Gillian Bickley. 2020.

Heart to Heart: Poems, by Patty Ho. 2010.

H/ERO/T/IC BOOK (translation from Macedonian), by Marta Markoska. 2020.

Home, away, elsewhere, by Vaughan Rapatahana. 2011.

Hong Kong Growing Pains, by Jon Ng. 2020.

Immortelle and bhandaaraa poems,
by Lelawattee Manoo-Rahming. 2011.

In vitro, by Laura Solomon. 2nd ed. 2014.

Irreverent poems for pretentious people, by Henrik Hoeg. 2016.

The layers between (essays and poems), by Celia Claase. 2015.

Of leaves & ashes, by Patty Ho. 2016.

Life Lines, by Shahilla Shariff. 2011.

Moving house and other poems from Hong Kong,
by Gillian Bickley. 2005.

Over the Years: Selected Collected Poems, 1972-2015,
by Gillian Bickley. 2017.

Painting the borrowed house: poems, by Kate Rogers. 2008.

Perceptions, by Gillian Bickley. 2012.

Poems from the Wilderness, by Jack Mayer. 2020.

Rain on the pacific coast, by Elbert Siu Ping Lee. 2013.

refrain, by Jason S. Polley. 2010.

Savage Charm, by Ahmed Elbeshlawy. 2019.

Shadow play, by James Norcliffe. 2012.

Shadows in deferment, by Birgit Bunzel Linder. 2013.

Shifting sands, by Deepa Vanjani. 2016.

Sightings: a collection of poetry, with an essay, 'communicating poems',
by Gillian Bickley. 2007.

Smoked pearl: poems of Hong Kong and beyond,
by Akin Jeje (Akinsola Olufemi Jeje). 2010.

Of symbols misused, by Mary-Jane Newton. 2011.

The Hummingbird Sometimes Flies Backwards, by D.J. Hamilton. 2019.

The Year of the Apparitions, by José Manuel Sevilla. 2020.

Uncharted Waters, by Paola Caronni. 2021.

Unlocking, by Mary-Jane Newton. 2014.

Violet, by Carolina Ilica. 2019.

Wonder, lust & itchy feet, by Sally Dellow. 2011.

POETRY ANTHOLOGIES
Published by Proverse Hong Kong

Mingled voices: the international Proverse Poetry Prize anthology 2016, edited by Gillian and Verner Bickley. 2017.

Mingled voices 2: the international Proverse Poetry Prize anthology 2017, edited by Gillian and Verner Bickley. 2018.

Mingled voices 3: the international Proverse Poetry Prize anthology 2018, edited by Gillian and Verner Bickley. 2019.

Mingled voices 4: the international Proverse Poetry Prize anthology 2019, edited by Gillian and Verner Bickley. 2020.

Mingled voices 5: the international Proverse Poetry Prize anthology 2020, edited by Gillian and Verner Bickley. 2021.

Mingled voices 6: the international Proverse Poetry Prize anthology 2021, edited by Gillian and Verner Bickley. 2022. *(Scheduled)*

FIND OUT MORE ABOUT PROVERSE AUTHORS, BOOKS, EVENTS AND LITERARY PRIZES

Visit our website: <http://www.proversepublishing.com>
Visit our distributor's website: www.cup.cuhk.edu.hk
Follow us on Twitter: twitter.com/Proversebooks
"Like" us on www.facebook.com/ProversePress

Request our free E-Newsletter
Send your request to info@proversepublishing.com.

Availability
Available in Hong Kong and world-wide from
our Hong Kong based distributor,
the Chinese University of Hong Kong Press,
The Chinese University of Hong Kong, Shatin, NT,
Hong Kong SAR, China.
See the Proverse page on the CUHKP website:
<https://cup.cuhk.edu.hk/Proversehk>

All titles are available from Proverse Hong Kong,
http://www.proversepublishing.com

Most titles can be ordered online from amazon
(various countries).

Stock-holding retailers
Hong Kong (CUHKP, Bookazine)
Canada (Elizabeth Campbell Books)
Andorra (Llibreria La Puça, La Llibreria)

Orders may be made from bookshops
in the UK and elsewhere.

Ebooks
Most of our titles are available also as Ebooks.

www.ingramcontent.com/pod-product-compliance
Ingram Content Group UK Ltd.
Pitfield, Milton Keynes, MK11 3LW, UK
UKHW022007190726
13853UKWH00004B/1780